Forty Years of Advice

Philip Wilkerson

Dedication

This book is dedicated to my incredible wife, Maggie Wilkerson, the love of my life. Without you, none of this would be possible. You are, without a doubt, the best thing that has happened to me in my forty years of living. Your unwavering support, love, and partnership have shaped me in ways words cannot fully express.

I also dedicate this to my sons, Bennett and Miles Wilkerson. Being your father has been my life's most rewarding and challenging role. I am beyond proud of the young men you two are becoming and am excited as I look forward to the men you will become.

Thank you all for being my constant inspiration.

Acknowledgments

This book would not have been possible without the guidance, inspiration, and support of many incredible individuals and communities in my life.

To all the mentors who have shaped my journey—your wisdom and encouragement have provided me with a model of excellence and purpose. Thank you for your support and for paving the way for me to share my own story.

To my family and friends who have authored books—witnessing your accomplishments has been a profound source of inspiration. Reading your works has empowered me to translate my thoughts and experiences into writing, and for that, I am truly grateful.

To my George Mason University community—thank you for fostering an environment where I have thrived both as an employee and a student. The opportunities to learn, grow, and connect in this space have been transformative and deeply meaningful.

Finally, I want to honor the Black authors who came before me. Your words hold immense power, and your courage to share your stories and wisdom continues to resonate in profound ways. In a time when such voices are more vital than ever, I am humbled to contribute my own to the legacy you have built.

Thank you all for inspiring, uplifting, and motivating me to bring this book to life.

Contents

About the Author

Philip Wilkerson is an Employer Engagement Consultant at GMU Career Services. In this role, he serves as a liaison between employers and the GMU community, facilitating career opportunities such as jobs and internships for students, faculty, staff, and alumni. He oversees industries including Media, Entertainment, Journalism, Public Relations, Graphic Design, Sports & Recreation, Hospitality & Tourism, and Technology & Engineering.

Earlier in 2024, Philip was nominated for the National Association of Colleges and Employers (NACE) "Mentor of the Year" award in recognition of his leadership and exceptional support for the professional growth and advancement of his mentees across the country. In 2019, he was named "Employee of the Month" for GMU in September and has since received several honors, including being listed in the "Forty under 40" for GMU Black Alumni, the Northern Virginia "Forty under Forty" through the Leadership Center for Excellence, and the "ALX Chamber Forty under Forty." Additionally, he was awarded the "Pillar Award," which recognizes a GMU staff member who supports Black students.

Beyond his professional role, Philip serves as the faculty advisor for the Iota Alpha Chapter of Alpha Phi Alpha Fraternity, Inc., and the GMU NAACP chapter. In his free time, he hosts a podcast called Positive Philter, which focuses on well-being and personal development, and is actively involved in Toastmasters.

Philip is married to Maggie Wilkerson, LCSW (JMU Class of 2007, Social Work), and together they are proud parents to two sons, Bennett and Miles.

Foreword

Life has a way of surprising us. For me, it started on January 29, 1985, in Landstuhl, Germany, where I entered the world as a premature baby, weighing only 3 lbs—7 oz. The son of military parents—Colonel Philip Wilkerson Jr. and Lieutenant Colonel Carol James Wilkerson—I had no idea this was just the beginning of a life that would take me around the globe, across countless experiences, and through many lessons. As I approach the next chapter of my life, reflecting on forty years of growth, I am humbled and grateful for the journey.

Through these four decades, I've connected with a remarkable network of family and friends who have guided me, supported me, and shared their wisdom. In the spirit of embracing that guidance, I reached out to those closest to me as I prepared for this milestone. What follows is a collection of inspirational quotes, advice, and life lessons I've gathered over the years. Some of these gems come from people who wished to remain anonymous, while others were happy to be a part of this book. Together, they form a powerful tapestry of insight, love, and encouragement—perfect for anyone navigating their journey through life.

Whether reflecting on your experiences or seeking wisdom for the road ahead, I hope you find something in these pages that resonates with you. Forty Years of Advice is a snapshot of where I've been, what I've learned, and the remarkable people who have helped shape who I am today. I split this book up into four sections: (1) Advice and Words of wisdom from myself, (2) Words of Advice from my family, friends, colleagues, frat brothers, and others in my network, (3) quotes or poems of inspiration that others wanted to share with me, and (4) advice from Dr. Kenneth Shore. As I know him, Uncle Kenny was my late father-in-law's, Jeff Kirsch, cousin. Jeff was a father figure and mentor to me, so having Kenny's advice means a lot to me, and it is worth having a section dedicated to him with his advice.

Enjoy the journey through these words, and may they inspire you as they have inspired me.

— Philip Wilkerson III

PART I

Forty Simple, Yet Powerful Life Lessons I've Learned Along The Way

1. What if it all works out? Don't count yourself out before you even begin.

2. Say "thank you" consistently and genuinely. Gratitude fosters connection and respect.

3. Pause before speaking. Take a moment to gather your thoughts to ensure your words reflect your true intentions.

4. Ask for help. Seeking support is a sign of strength; no one succeeds alone.

5. Maintain a welcoming expression in public. Your demeanor affects how others perceive you, even if you're friendly.

6. Speak directly, not behind someone's back. Honest, face-to-face conversations build trust and integrity.

7. Prioritize your time. Time is your most valuable resource—you can't get it back once it's gone.

8. Don't put all your eggs in one basket. Diversify your options to minimize risks.

9. Set SMART goals. Make them Specific, Measurable, Achievable, Relevant, and Time-bound to ensure success.

10. Get enough sleep. It's essential for your health, focus, and overall well-being.

11. Enjoy life's small pleasures in moderation. Balance indulgence with responsibility.

12. Respect tradition but embrace change. Honor the past while staying open to innovation.

13. Surround yourself with inspiring people. Seek environments that challenge and elevate you.

14. Stay hydrated. Drinking plenty of water is crucial for your physical and mental health.

15. Own at least three suits. A black, gray, or navy suit is a timeless wardrobe essential.

16. Face your problems head-on. Avoiding them only delays the inevitable; courage brings resolution.

17. Dance without worrying about how you look. Move freely and enjoy the moment.

18. Check in with your "strong" friends. They may not ask for help but still need support.

19. Read often. Books are transformative tools that feed your mind and expand your perspective.

20. Don't overcommit and underdeliver. Be realistic about your abilities and follow through on your promises.

21. Listen more than you talk. Focus on understanding rather than just responding.

22. Education is a gateway to opportunities. Engage both inside and outside the classroom to build connections.

23. Build a strong reputation. Your credibility and relationships often speak for you before you do.

24. Go for a walk. Movement sparks creativity—carry a notepad or phone to capture your ideas.

25. Don't wait to create. Start now; perfection comes with practice and persistence.

26. Repetition leads to improvement. Doing something repeatedly is the fastest way to get better.

27. True friends show up during tough times. Trust those who are there for you when it matters most.

28. Focus on the marriage, not just the wedding. A wedding is one day; a marriage is a lifelong partnership.

29. Always wear clean underwear. You never know when you might need help, and first impressions matter.

30. Never stop learning. Especially in technology, staying adaptable ensures you remain competitive.

31. Remember and spell people's names correctly. Names carry meaning and show respect.

32. Write handwritten notes. They leave a personal and lasting impression in the digital world.

33. Share struggles with trusted people. Not every issue needs to be public.

34. Life is short. Enjoy what you love while you can—stop overthinking.

35. Trust the timing of your life. Everything happens right on schedule.

36. Write down your goals. Focus intensely until you achieve your mission.

37. Be your own cheerleader. Hyping yourself is confidence, not arrogance—don't let anyone dim your light.

38. Speak up. Great ideas are wasted if they're not shared. Public speaking is an essential skill.

39. Fail forward. Embrace failure as a step toward growth and progress.

40. Learn something new every day. Every experience is an opportunity to grow.

PART II

Advice From My Friends

The question I asked my network: What is one piece of advice or wisdom you'd like to share as I approach 40?

"Self-care is imperative. As caregivers, we can sometimes forget to take care of ourselves. Remember to care for your emotional, physical, spiritual, and financial health." - Ty

"Celebrate the successes of others, even if you don't feel successful in your own life at that very moment. I've found that doing this has strengthened my community. That same community will be there during the highs and other learning moments." - Evan

"Always Trust Your A.S.S.

- Alignment

- Self-Mastery

- Service

Alignment of Purpose, People, and Places. If there's no alignment...you don't get involved.

Continue to improve to mastery in EVERYTHING that matters...and continue to grow. Even then.

Prioritize the service of others. After an interaction with Phil...do folks leave better?!?! If you serve well...the answer will be a resounding YES." - Mike Dorsey

"Always be intentional, set boundaries, and continue to hold yourself accountable to these!" - Chrissy Lawrence

"No one can make you feel inferior without your consent," said Eleanor Roosevelt. I have incorporated that lesson into my life. I used to give away my power by focusing on people-pleasing. I do not do that anymore. Life is short, and none of us knows how much time we have in this life. So I do not try so hard to make others like me, because that is a losing battle. The only person we can control is ourselves." - Maria Leonard Olsen

"Happy husbands are just as important as happy wives. There just isn't a clever jingle. Remember to make time for yourself too." - JB

"Be unapologetically YOU!" - Ann S.

"You only get one heart. Get yourself an ECG, echocardiogram, and calcium score. Know your family medical history." - Maryann Nason

"Put God first in all that you do. Seek Him for guidance, walk by faith, and, even in the presence of obstacles and heartbreak, He will lead you, guide you, and come through for you. He will make your enemies your footstool and will turn a negative into a blessing. You will not regret a life lived for God. May you be blessed! Happy 40th Birthday, Phil!!!" - Dannita Trice

"Be economically savvy: savings, retirement planning, college for kids. But also, relaxation, prayer, and joy." - Anonymous

"The learning never stops. It's one big ride!" - Debbie Z.

"Take care of yourself. At age 40, what you eat and how much you exercise start to really matter and become more important with each passing year." - Lynne Strang

"Invest in you! As the world becomes a bit unpredictable, there is no better time than now to abandon what we 'think' we should do and double down on our passions. Because after all, it is passion that helps to move us forward." - Patrick Harris II

"As someone who turned 40 earlier this year, focusing on one's mental and physical health is important. Find time to take care of these things and do what works best for you!" - Anonymous

"This is a time to focus on personal growth, family, friendships, and passions." - Prof. Rodger Smith

"Chance encounters can sometimes lead to unexpected outcomes that change our career and life pathways. Embrace these interactions like a sponge, soaking up others' advice, suggestions, and guidance. While it's unnecessary to act on every piece of feedback, imagine the possibilities if even 1% leads to a positive short- or long-term outcome." - Luis F. Mercado, Jr.

"Good writing is rewriting." - Michael Don

"Stay on your barber's calendar every 2-3 weeks. Maintain a clean hairline and trim the naps." - John Busby

"Travel. Don't wait. Go on whatever budget you have, whether in your state or internationally. Also, get outside every day. Walk as much as possible." - Anonymous

"Gratitude is, to me, such an important part of life. Truly feeling grateful for the people in your life and any other things you are grateful for - and expressing that - is a win-win. It makes you feel good, as well as those around you. Can't lose with gratitude!" - Jen

"Be more interested than interesting, be kind to your future self, and do good deeds! May all your wishes come true, and wish for more wishes. Happy Birthday, Philip!" - David Meltzer

"If you don't learn to find joy in the snow, you will have less joy in your life and precisely the same amount of snow." - Sam Hardman

"Life gets fast and noisy. It is up to you to create calm for yourself and your family—enough calm to invest carefully and purposefully into relationships that really matter." - Jerry Stayton

"Your best years are always ahead of you." - Ameer Baker

"Here's to more alignment, more abundance, more opportunities, and every good thing you deserve." - Keyah

"Life is fleeting. Nothing is more important than the moment you're experiencing. Appreciate it, revel in it, and most importantly, be grateful for it!" - Hakeem Osman

"No matter what happens in your life, never give up." - Anonymous

"I learned something from a college friend that has proved true in most circumstances: Go strong, and the world will go with you. Be confident, act like you know what you're doing and what you're about, and most people will follow your lead!" - Scott Kyles

"Learn to say no to things. As you approach the big four-0, it's important to protect and preserve your peace over anything else. It's okay to say no to things you don't want to do." - Dee

"Buy the fancy coffee maker if you haven't already. Life is too short for bad coffee; you deserve the upgrade." - Anonymous

"That perfection does not exist, and that the moment we accept that truth, we can free ourselves from so much heartache, stress, etc." - Erin

"Let go of everything that doesn't support the next version of yourself and your life." - Zoa Sharin

"Learn to stretch and protect your back before, during, and after pretty much everything. Knee pain is rough, but back pain will take you out. A few basic back exercises go a long way when you need them." - Kristin from Work

"Keep being your uplifting self, but never be afraid to ask for help!" - Sophia Lopez

"Don't feel pressured to grow old and wise. Maturing is a good thing, but life becomes a lot less fun if you stop being fun." - Ilia Sheikholeslami

"40 is the new 30. You're never out of your prime unless you think that you are." - Devin

"Buy some bitcoin. Though it is not the asset of today, it definitely is the asset of the future. Your descendants will be so proud of you!" - Jermaine

"How about two pieces of wisdom that have come to serve me well?

1) No matter how outrageous it sounds, nothing in life is inherently positive or negative; it simply is, it simply occurred, is a fact, and must be experienced. We can decide what it will be: motivational, insightful, an opportunity—or demoralizing, useless, or defeating.

2) Another counterintuitive piece of advice: Do not walk through life with your fist clenched, trying to protect that which you deem of value too aggressively without discernment. While a closed hand prevents someone from taking something of value from you, it also prevents someone from giving you something of value. Giving as freely as you are blessed is a blessing for you and other people; it's an exercise in gratitude and appreciation for your blessings in life, regardless of the size of the blessing."
- Grealin C. Kimbrough

"Continue to live life at your own pace. Celebrate everything!" - Uncle Mo

"Surround yourself with wise counsel who will speak love and truth. You'll go farther in life with people who lift you, encourage you, and help you be the best version of yourself." - Christie Michals

"The only thing you should worry about is your attitude." - Alexander G. J.

"Continue to be the man that you are, and don't put so much pressure on yourself." - Anonymous

"Continue to press forward and put into the generation behind you, so that you contribute to their race." - Rob Blackwell Jr.

"Be completely transparent at all times. Make sure everyone you speak to clearly understands your expectations. If your expectations are not clearly stated, those close to you may not meet them. This can lead to disappointment and resentment on your side. Make them clear at all times to avoid this, as it can lead to bad choices on your part." - Anonymous

"Age is but a number and this is still your prime life! As you get older, it is more and more important to lead the next generation. This is something that I believe you are doing well in, and I just encourage you never to change and keep doing what you do!" - Anonymous

"BE KIND!" - CJ

"Cherish the opportunity to pause, breathe deeply, and reflect. When I look to my parents and people who have lived to and beyond 40, they wish they would have taken it easier some days, reflected more often, and taken in each moment with more gratitude and genuine care." - Anonymous

"Trust the process!" - Anonymous

"Take your life one day at a time, and don't make decisions when you're mad." - Diana Mendez

"Always prioritize your family and make time for your children, regardless of how far in your career you go or how busy you may be." - Anonymous

"With your experience working in numerous fields, it would be necessary to continue to inspire those around you as you have more to share with others." - Anonymous

"Be yourself because everyone else is taken." - Duane Bailey

"Be kind to yourself and others." - Anonymous

"Success is not measured by the heights we reach alone but by the foundation we build through the love of family and the strength of community—each victory reflects those who uplifted us along the way." - Anonymous

"As the unofficial Mayor of Mason, you've got to continue being a role model to your kids and the community. So keep your health first; in these years of your life, it'll be important to prioritize health to maintain a good, long life." - Anonymous

"Spend as much time outside as you can, especially in the morning! Daylight is critical for keeping our internal clock in sync. Disrupted circadian rhythms are associated with many health issues, including depression, diabetes, heart disease, cancer, and dementia." - Anonymous

"Stay motivated!" - Anonymous

"Keep showing up as yourself. Many of us wear different masks with different communities, but you always appear and come across as an authentic Phil every day." - Anonymous

"Don't sweat the small stuff!" - Anonymous

"Everything leading up to 40 is just research. Your REAL life starts at 40. Dedicate your life to mastering yourself." - Anonymous

"Continue to cultivate those relationships. You have been a blessing to everyone. Finally, never stop learning or striving for new goals." - Anonymous

"Accept this moment as it is. So much of our suffering is caused by wishing things are different than they are." - Anonymous

"Spend as much time doing things you love—playing games, working out, traveling. Eat lots of great food and explore the unknown. When you get older, things slow down, your body changes, and you're unable to do, eat, or enjoy all of the things you once did." - Michelle Blackston

"Kindness and empathy go a long way; work extremely hard for your goals."

"Always follow your heart and passion, and the money will come!"

"Ensure you are enjoying your ONE life; however, what are your plans for retirement, and will your family be set up for success 20 years from now? Know your end goals!" - Jermaine Jenkins

"Embrace your age. It isn't about what you've left behind; it's about what you have ahead of you." - Amanda Dixon

"Keep having fun and live life to the fullest! Age is nothing but a number!"

"Always try to plan since life moves fast, but live every day enjoying the present moment that you find yourself in." - Clement Lupton

"Take a break when you can and make time to prioritize yourself (and your family). The hustle will always be there, but making memories and giving yourself room to wind down is key. You are a wonderful and inspiring person—I love seeing how hard you work, and everyone notices. Thank you for always showing kindness—it matters and is always appreciated."

"Embrace aging. Use the wisdom you've gained over the years to your advantage. Enjoy exploring new challenges; you might find something interesting about yourself that you never knew!" - Sean

"Life is meant to be lived; do so with purpose." - David Atkins

"Organize priorities the way they make sense to you, not based on what someone says you should do."

"Life never gets easier. When you think you've got it all figured out, life throws you another curve. Don't live for a future in which life is easier, because then you will always be searching for the next thing, break, or solution. You will always look to the future and not live in the moment. Instead, live to make yourself someone who can handle whatever comes your way." - Angie Hattery

"Time is the only currency we spend without knowing the balance. Spend time with those who energize you." - Marcy

"It's nice to look back and learn, but it's imperative to see forward and do." - Mike W.

"Everyone is just trying to do the best they can with what they've got at the moment... and fewer people are paying attention to us than we thought all along... do what you like, improve what you want to improve, and don't worry about anyone else!" - Sean Schofield

"Be where your feet are."

"Service comes from sacrifice and suffering." - Philip L. Wilkerson Jr.

"Nobody will like what you do!" - Philip Linwood Wilkerson Jr.

"I don't need to trust you; you need to trust yourself." - Bennett Wilkerson

"Leadership is service. You make sacrifices to serve others which cause suffering." - Philip L. Wilkerson Jr.

"A degree without a plan is just an expensive receipt." - Trovon Williams

"Live a life of giving and loving." - David Anderson

"Prayerfully be alert and aware of everything. Read the ROOM, understand what you are seeing, your actions, and reactions." - Bro. Mike Freeman

"Stay positive and keep shining your light!" - Nick M.

"To be present in the moment and appreciate your current blessings, rather than hoping for new, better things in the future. You are a wonderful husband, father, son, and friend, and I am so proud of you!" - Maggie

"Keep dreaming big and staying focused on your goals. Remember—life's a marathon, not a sprint! Never lose the positivity and optimism that makes you Positive Phil (ter)!" - Hermana

"Live boldly, life is precious and you need to savor every moment."

"Embrace it and own it! Getting older is actually a privilege that many don't embrace!" - Carlos Stewart

"40 is that number where you are old enough to know better but still young enough to experience what life has to offer. Prepare for your financial future and that of your heirs, take your health seriously, make all appointments, and take time to enjoy your hobbies and interests." - Mark S. Tillman

"In everyday life, a forecaster's certainty about precipitation forming or moving into an area translates most closely to the level of confidence someone has in a prediction or outcome; essentially, how sure they are that something will happen based on available information.

As you approach your 40th birthday, your measured thoughts, actions, and views will serve as the keys to life. There's a 40% chance that you've experienced most things yet to come, but there's a 60% you haven't. That is OK!

Just like a weather forecast might say there's a '60% chance of rain,' you might say, 'I'm 60% confident that this project will be successful.'

With rain comes growth, and growth begets pains and struggles! Embrace each rainy day with the same joyous purpose as you do when the sun shines bright and the moon is full!

Frat, your heart is full of love and passion. Your willingness to hold open your hands to not only receive your recognized blessings, but you're just as willing to reach back to assist others growing just as vibrantly as you do!

Congratulations on your 40th trip around this 'interesting' world. May your journey through the next 60% be just as rewarding! Peace and blessings! Always'06!" - Bro. Jeffery D. Jackson

"It is everyone's first time at life! Not everyone is going to have their stuff perfectly figured out, and those who insist that they do are only putting on a façade to make themselves feel better. It is also perfectly normal and okay to change directions from what you initially thought you wanted and what was best for you. Give yourself grace as you navigate your journey, and grant yourself the permission to make mistakes and change your mind—it's your first time doing this, so don't demand perfection when what you're really seeking is peace!" - Alaina

"Continue to practice gratitude. There are so many people who didn't make it to their 40s. Count this as a blessing and continue to pour into others." - EJ Jones

"You are a good man, with a genuine heart. I would say don't worry about the outside noise. Take care of yourself and your family. Your energy is good for the world! I love you, brother!" - Lewis Forrest, II.

"You cannot change the past, but you can always look towards the future." - Obum E.

"Continue to be a dope soul to others around you; you inspire many around you." - Tim/T.H.

"Celebrate your glows and learn from your grows!!" - Fred W. Scott

"I've been reading a lot of books about staying centered and focused. In *The Happiness Project*, Gretchen Rubin wrote, 'It's about living in the moment and appreciating the smallest things. Surrounding yourself with the things that inspire you and letting go of the obsessions that want to take over your mind. It is a daily struggle sometimes and hard work, but happiness begins with your own attitude and how you look at the world.'

Mel Robbins just released a book called *The Let Them Theory*. She shared on a recent podcast, 'Stop wasting your time and energy having negative thoughts, opinions, and judgments of other people and start putting that power, time, and energy back into yourself.'

In addition to being more patient, appreciative, and self-reflective, I am also working on my boundaries and reactions. I now embrace that the word 'No' is a full sentence in response to a question. There is no need for explanation or defense." - Kara Stamper

"The wisdom gained from experiences opens doors to new enlightenment." - Brian Boles

"As you near 40, my advice is to embrace your youthful spirit. While many might see 40 as a milestone of 'older age,' I encourage you to stay vibrant and active. Let the wisdom you've gained guide you in continuing to uplift and enrich your community, and you'll be proud of the way you launch into this exciting new chapter." - Junias

"Keep spreading joy and positivity the way that you do. Your love for others is apparent, and that will continue to sustain you. Other things, more or less free medical knowledge, but NOT advice because I am not a doctor (yet): Continue to keep your brain engaged and lift weights to maintain muscle mass. You're not lifting for ego; you're lifting for function so you can squat when you're 80 or bend over. Walk 20 minutes a day and put on a podcast or walk with God." - Sean Diment

"As we grow up, we realize it's less important to have lots of friends and more important to have real ones." - Jeannie

"Live in your main character era! Be ambitious, truly be goal-oriented, and put no pressure on yourself to appease others." - Joseph Deluna

"Keep up with that boy!!!" - Tom

"Don't take yourself too seriously. Shouldn't be a problem."
- Moose

"Be open to curiosity, discovery, and your emotions. By prematurely cutting off options, you never know what could have been. Learning and a growth mindset will help you see what's possible."

"Enjoy every minute (if you weren't already!)" - Mom of Moose boys!

"Don't get bored with routine success." - Chris Preston

"You may be 40, but you have the heart of a 21-year-old. Never lose sight of that." - Cheese

"There is a great joy and comfort in being a lifelong seeker of wisdom and knowledge; and even more when you may pass it on to another." - Austin A.

"Practice gratitude and self-compassion and share this with the people you love." - Joan

"**Know What's Precious:** We have a limited amount of time each day, week, month, and year. Too often, it's wasted on others' agendas and expectations. With just one life, be discerning about how you spend your time.

Be Bold: Have the courage to express your desires and take action, even when others hesitate. There is a deficit in social courage—deviate.

Rethink Regret: You'll find more pain in inaction than in making mistakes. Accept the regrets that come with taking personal and social risks to improve your life and the lives of others." - Todd Kashdan

"Shoot your shot. Do things with confidence and use all the lessons from the past to propel you further."

"Be the age you are! Forty IS not the new 20 or 30; it's 40. When you become 41, don't long to be something you're not. Embrace 40 as a 40-year-old and eliminate any regrets from your past or fears for your future. I got this from my dad, and I'm passing it on to you!" - Sam

"Consider cycling, hiking, or running as something to add to your hobby list. Health is wealth, my brother." - Hugh

"1. Joke: Don't think of turning 40 as getting old, but think of it as you getting better at scheduling naps and forgetting why you walked into a room.

2. Serious: Life is only lifing when you let it life, but life isn't truly lifing if you're too afraid to let life not life the way life is meant to life." - Yves Sayid Laurent

"Time is your most valuable asset; use it wisely."

"Go forth inspired to change the world." - Keith Green

"Never forget to touch the grass." - Courtney B.

"Being healthy can feel uncomfortable when you've always existed in survival mode. Achievement can feel necessary until you realize that valuing yourself and learning how to listen to your body is the most important and healthiest milestone you can reach in your life." - Tibi

"At the age of 40 comes an opportunity for rebirth. Wisdom and experience, now more than ever, guide your actions and outlook on life. You are better equipped to receive blessings and to be a blessing for others." - Roderick Blount

"Work to keep your friendships vibrant and healthy. It gets harder as the years go by to make new friends. But also, don't be afraid of establishing and strengthening new connections. By the way, fifties are the new forties. You'll see what I mean in 10 years. Enjoy the ride!"

PART III

Inspirational Quotes, Poems, Or Sayings That Resonate With Others

"After a while, the noise blends into the background, and you learn to function in spite of it." - Unknown

"Be a good man." - My Grandfather (Evan)

James 2:17 states, "Thus also faith by itself, if it does not have works, is dead."

"No one can make you feel inferior without your consent." - Eleanor Roosevelt

"The hardest challenge is to be yourself in a world where everyone is trying to make you be somebody else." - E. E. Cummings

"Being right is a low bar to set." - Unknown

"The blessing of the Lord, it maketh rich, and he addeth no sorrow with it." - Proverbs 10:22

"Never give in to despair. Trust that your angels and ancestors are always working for your best." - Unknown

"Learn to forgive yourself again, and again, and again!" - Sheldon B. Kopp

"Don't Sweat the Small Stuff. And it's all Small Stuff." - Title of a book by Richard Carlson

"Do what you love. The money will follow." - Marsha Sinetar

"Be not afraid of growing slowly; be afraid of standing still." - Unknown (message found on a fortune cookie in Luis F. Mercado Jr.'s wallet)

"Those who say it can't be done are usually interrupted by others doing it." - James Baldwin

"Do all the good you can, by all the means you can, in all the ways you can, in all the places you can, at all the times you can, to all the people you can, as long as ever you can." - John Wesley

"The elevator to success is broken. You'll have to use the stairs... one step at a time." - Joe Girard

"A ship in a harbor is safe, but that is not what ships are built for." - John A. Shedd

"Be curious, not judgmental." - Attributed to an advice column written by Marguerite and Marshall Shearer

Don't Quit By Edgar Albert Guest

When things go wrong, as they sometimes will,

when the road you're trudging seems all uphill,

when the funds are low and the debts are high,

and you want to smile but you have to sigh,

when care is pressing you down a bit—rest if you must, but don't you quit.

Life is queer with its twists and turns,

as every one of us sometimes learns.

And many a fellow turns about

when he might have won had he stuck it out.

Don't give up though the pace seems slow—you may succeed with another blow.

Often the goal is nearer than it seems to a faint and faltering man;

often the struggler has given up

when he might have captured the victor's cup;

and he learned too late when the night came down,

how close he was to the golden crown.

Success is failure turned inside out—the silver tint of the clouds of doubt,

and you never can tell how close you are,

it may be near when it seems afar;

so stick to the fight when you're hardest hit—it's when things seem worst, you must not quit.

"Our deepest fear is not that we are inadequate. Our deepest fear is that we are powerful beyond measure. It is our light, not our darkness, that most frightens us. We ask ourselves, 'Who am I to be brilliant, gorgeous, talented, fabulous?' Actually, who are you not to be?

You are a child of God. Your playing small does not serve the world. There is nothing enlightened about shrinking so that other people won't feel insecure around you. We are all meant to shine, as children do.

We were born to make manifest the glory of God that is within us. It's not just in some of us; it's in everyone. And as we let our own light shine, we unconsciously give other people permission to do the same. As we are liberated from our own fear, our presence automatically liberates others." - Marianne Williamson

"Aim at heaven, and you will get earth thrown in. Aim at earth, and you get neither." - C.S. Lewis

"I think, therefore, I am."

Explanation: We are whoever we perceive ourselves to be, and we should always regard ourselves highly in our minds and hearts before we can expect to be regarded as such from the outside.

"In this world, you either crank that Soulja Boy, or it cranks you." - Soulja Boy

"In all our deeds, the proper value and respect for time determine success or failure."

"You can't save time. You can only spend it, but you can spend it wisely or foolishly." - Benjamin Hoff, The Tao of Pooh

"Work is work, but work ain't life. Spend time doing your best job and making money, but don't give work and money all of your time. Time is precious. Spend as much time as you can with the people that mean the most to you."

"Failure is a feeling long before it becomes an actual result. It's vulnerability that breeds with self-doubt and then is escalated, often deliberately, by fear." - Michelle Obama

"Sometimes quiet is violent." - Tyler Joseph (song lyric from Car Radio by Twenty One Pilots)

"We're all just doing the best we can, and that's enough."

"Don't miss out on life trying to get it together."

"F' the haters. :) "

"What is faith without doubt?"

"The righteous person may have many troubles, but the Lord delivers him from them all." - Psalms 34:19

"You are never too old to set another goal or to dream a new dream." - C.S. Lewis

"Treat Yourself!" - Invictus

"Whatever you are, be a good one. Wherever you are, be all there."

"I love to sing and play the piano. When I tell people I can't play the piano and I have a terrible voice, they assume I can't play or sing anything. It's the opposite—I can play and sing anything I want." - Tig Notaro

Poem by Maggie Millner

Life is to be lived.

Some people like to walk on the yellow brick road. While others like to build it!

Don't sweat the small stuff.

It's not the age that defines the person but rather the things they learned from their time.

"The only 'L' I take is a LESSON! I never lose; I only LEARN! There's value in the experience, so trust the process! Understand which life scoreboard you are viewing based on your current situation. It's not about the win... it's about the learned values."

"And you know who I wanna thank? I wanna thank me! For believing in me and doing what they said I could not do." - Niecy Nash, winning her much-deserved Emmy

"The coward dies a thousand deaths; the brave but one. The man who first said that was probably a coward. He knew a great deal about cowards but nothing about the brave. The brave die perhaps two thousand deaths if they're intelligent. They simply don't mention them."

"What you tell yourself, you will become." - Dr. Ivan Joseph

"Good is the enemy of great." - David Foster

"Clear is kind." - Brené Brown

"Ask for a job, and you will get advice. Ask for advice, and you will get a job." - Nick

"We are people to be loved, not used." - Terry Crews

"Give the world your best, live full, and die empty." - Les Brown

"Confidence is the willingness to try." - Mel Robbins

"The more aware we become, the more we recognize how responsible we must be." - Unknown

"Might as well have fun 'cause your happiness is done when your goose is cooked." - Outkast

"Put all of your extra money in Bitcoin."

"Don't be afraid to try something new and fail the first time! Ask more questions and for help when you need it!"

"Mercy is for the weak."

"Be the hammer, not the nail."

"Clear eyes, full hearts, can't lose."

"I would rather be an optimist and be wrong than be a pessimist and be right." - Unknown

"Fine: I would say, there are different steps to learning.

- Unconscious incompetence: You don't know what something is, and you can't do it.
- Conscious incompetence: You know about it but you can't do it.
- Conscious competence: You know it, and you can do it.

Don't get frustrated and give up in step 1. And just because you're not an expert at something, if you love it, keep doing it. You like to play basketball, but there are only 490 professional basketball players working today. If Kobe Bryant told you you suck, should you stop playing basketball because you can't compete with him?"

"How we treat others is how we treat ourselves. If you are kind to others, you will be kind to yourself."

"God hides treasures in the trials."

"You are the fathers of your community."

"Take the gifts of this hour."

"You don't change your life because someone told you to. You change your life because you want to." - Jon Daly

"Iron sharpens iron."

"Over my family, I will put you first." - Khalid (shot down)

"Building a sustainable product isn't just about what you're selling, it's who is selling it. I'm not buying what I can't take seriously."

"The enemy is fear. We think it is hate; but, it is fear." - Gandhi

"Wise men say forgiveness is divine, but never pay full price for late pizza." - Michelangelo (TMNT)

"How you live will determine the attendance of your funeral. Live a life that will pack a church." - Adrian

"With great power comes great responsibility." - Spider-Man

"The best you're going to do in anything is when you're having a good time." - Bill Murray

"Jealousy leads to murder." - Dateline

"I have a dream that one day little Black boys and girls will be holding hands with little white boys and girls." - Martin Luther King Jr.

"All growth depends on activity. There is no development physically or intellectually without effort, and effort means work." - Calvin Coolidge

"Chancletas!"

"Pessimism leads to weakness, optimism to power." - William James

"Action is the precursor to motivation." - Isaiah 41:10

"Fear not! For I am with you. Be not dismayed, for I am thy God. I will strengthen you and help you; I will uphold you with my righteous right hand." - Romans 8:31

"What then shall we say in response to these things? If God is for us, who can be against us?"

"I love America more than any other country in this world, and, exactly for this reason, I insist on the right to criticize her perpetually." - James A. Baldwin

"Kindness is the best medicine." - Jennifer Klenzman

"Walking in your calling may confuse other people who were not on the phone line when God told you what He told you."

"There will always be people who identify an area for you to improve on and not highlight the areas where you're an asset to them."

"Rest allows me to do what I love." - Unknown

"If there is no struggle, there is no progress. Those who profess to favor freedom, and yet depreciate agitation, are men who want crops without plowing up the ground." - Frederick Douglass

"No one needs to fail for me to succeed." - Shyne

"I stopped letting the world determine my worth a long time ago. The world will always undervalue you, criticize you, and consider you overrated. I've learned that I can only find my true value when I set my own standards." - Me

"Epitaph" by Merrit Malloy

When I die,

Give what's left of me away

To children

And old men that wait to die.

And if you need to cry,

Cry for your brother

Walking the street beside you.

And when you need me,

Put your arms

Around anyone

And give them

What you need to give to me.

I want to leave you something,

Something better

Than words

Or sounds.

Look for me

In the people I've known

Or loved.

And if you cannot give me away,

At least let me live on in your eyes

And not your mind.

You can love me most

By letting

Hands touch hands,

By letting bodies touch bodies,

And by letting go

Of children

That need to be free.

Love doesn't die,

People do.

So, when all that's left of me

Is love,

Give me away.

Cat's In The Cradle by Harry Chapin

My child arrived just the other day,

He came to the world in the usual way.

But there were planes to catch and bills to pay,

He learned to walk while I was away.

And he was talkin' 'fore I knew it, and as he grew,

He'd say, *"I'm gonna be like you, Dad,*

You know I'm gonna be like you."

And the cat's in the cradle and the silver spoon,

Little boy blue and the man on the moon.

"When you comin' home, Dad?"

"I don't know when, but we'll get together then.

You know we'll have a good time then."

My son turned ten just the other day.

He said, "*Thanks for the ball, Dad, come on, let's play.*

Can you teach me to throw?" I said, "*Not today.*

I got a lot to do." He said, "*That's okay.*"

And he walked away, but his smile never dimmed

And said, "*I'm gonna be like him, yeah,*

You know I'm gonna be like him."

And the cat's in the cradle and the silver spoon,

Little boy blue and the man on the moon.

"*When you comin' home, Dad?*"

"*I don't know when, but we'll get together then.*

You know we'll have a good time then."

Well, he came from college just the other day,

So much like a man I just had to say,

"*Son, I'm proud of you, can you sit for a while?*"

He shook his head and then said with a smile,

"*What I'd really like, Dad, is to borrow the car keys.*

See you later, can I have them please?"

45

And the cat's in the cradle and the silver spoon,

Little boy blue and the man on the moon.

"When you comin' home, son?"
"I don't know when, but we'll get together then, Dad.

You know we'll have a good time then."

I've long since retired, my son's moved away.

I called him up just the other day.

I said, *"I'd like to see you if you don't mind."*

He said, *"I'd love to, Dad, if I can find the time.*

You see, my new job's a hassle and the kid's got the flu,

But it's sure nice talking to you, Dad.

It's been sure nice talking to you."

And as I hung up the phone, it occurred to me,

He'd grown up just like me.

My boy was just like me.

And the cat's in the cradle and the silver spoon,

Little boy blue and the man on the moon.

"When you comin' home, son?"

"I don't know when, but we'll get together then, Dad.

We're gonna have a good time then."

"Life has no limitations except the ones you make." - Les Brown

"Great minds discuss ideas; average minds discuss events; small minds discuss people." - Eleanor Roosevelt

"The greatness of a community is most accurately measured by the compassionate actions of its members." - CSK

"Falling down is an accident, but staying down is a choice..." - Unknown

"Keep your face to the sunshine, and you cannot see the shadows." - Helen Keller

"Until the lion learns how to write, every story will glorify the hunter."

"Mind over matter: Those who mind, don't matter, and those who matter, don't mind."

"Life doesn't happen to you, it happens for you." - Tony Robbins

"Sighhhhhhhhhh..."

"The most precious gift that we offer others is our presence." - Thich Nhat Hanh

"You are the author of your own life story." - Susan Young

"I hope the people that I hate always know that I hate them. Because I want the people that I love to know that I love them. And you can't have it both ways." - Nikki Giovanni

"Pain is your friend; it lets you know you're still alive."

"You can't make people love you, but you can make them fear you."

"The only way to know how strong you are is to keep testing your limits."

"Do or do not. There is no try." - Yoda

"You only have one life, and it's a short one, so work hard now and enjoy life, plus your family."

"All that is gold does not glitter, not all those who wander are lost; the old that is strong does not wither, deep roots are not reached by the frost." - Bilbo Baggins, *The Lord of the Rings*

"The days are long, but the years are short."

"If a man has not found something worth dying for, he is not fit to live." - Dr. Martin Luther King Jr.

"Do not go where the path may lead; go instead where there is no path and leave a trail." - Ralph Waldo Emerson

"Count your age by friends, not years. Count your life by smiles, not tears." - John Lennon

"It is what it is. Because of this, embrace what you have to face in life and navigate it to your benefit."

"It will never get easier. What happens is you handle hard better.

Make yourself a person that handles hard well, not someone who's waiting for the easy."

- Kara Lawson, Duke Women's Basketball Coach

"I always go to Helen Keller: life is a daring adventure or nothing at all. Security is an illusion."

"Don't give up, don't ever give up." - Jimmy V

"100% of the shots you don't take don't go in!"

"I am a dreamer. I am indeed a practical dreamer. I do not dream of useless nothings. Insofar as possible, I convert my dreams into reality." - Gandhi

"Keep your head up; you can't see your blessings looking down."

"The future belongs to those who believe in the beauty of their dreams." - Eleanor Roosevelt

"Yesterday is history. Tomorrow is a mystery. Today is a gift—that's why they call it the present."

"Be yourself; everyone else is already taken." - Oscar Wilde

"If serving is beneath you, leadership is beyond you!" - Doug Thorpe

"The Aggregation of Marginal Gain:

The philosophy of getting up each day searching for ways to get better at everything we do and everything we touch by using marginal means.

The greatest changes or positive matriculation in life do not have to be massive overhauls. Sometimes it's changing environment, the manner in which one speaks, mindset, and community.

Who you run with determines what you run to. Free your mind and allow yourself to grow like green leaves."

"When life is good, say thank you.

When life is bitter, say thank you and grow."

"This is the beginning of a new day. You can use it as you will. You can waste it or use it for good.

What you do today is important because you are exchanging your life for it.

When tomorrow comes, this day will be gone forever, and in its place will be something you left behind. Make sure it's something good."

"You'll never know until you try—if the worst thing they can say is no, you have fewer limits to throw your darts out there and see what lands.

Also, my mantra: 'Do it scared!'"

"It may not be your fault, but it's now your problem. So much in life is a result of the actions of others, but it's on us to face and tackle those problems, especially the problems of those who are more vulnerable than we are."

"Give yourself grace, have peace in all you do, push yourself, because you are built for what's ahead."

"When you're backed against the wall, break the goddamn thing down." - Harvey Specter

"The time is always right to do what is right." - Dr. Martin L. King Jr.

"Integrity is choosing courage over comfort, choosing what is right over what is fun, fast, or easy; and choosing to practice our values rather than simply professing them." - Brené Brown

"To love ourselves and support each other in the process of becoming real is perhaps the greatest single act of daring greatly." - Brené Brown

"You are imperfect, you are wired for struggle, but you are worthy of love and belonging. Vulnerability is the birthplace of innovation, creativity, and change." - Brené Brown

"The ultimate measure of a man is not where he stands in moments of comfort and convenience, but where he stands at times of challenge and controversy." - Martin Luther King Jr.

"Seek the Kingdom of God above all else, and live righteously, and He will give you everything you need." - Matthew 6:33 (NLT)

"Life is not measured by the number of breaths we take, but by the moments that take our breath away."

"It will be aight."

"Hope is not a method." - General Gordon R. Sullivan

"Every day is a chance to begin again. Don't focus on the failures of yesterday. Start today with positive thoughts and expectations. Start today with the intention of doing good things. You got this!"

"The minute you settle for less than you deserve, you get even less than you settled for."

"Everything in moderation, including moderation." - Oscar Wilde

"Look forward to the anxiety of uncertainty." - Mike Tomlin

"We have to be like water. When we are poured, we conform to the vessel we fall into. Stay fluid."

"Chaucer wrote this about the Clerk in his prologue:

'But al that he myghte of his freendes hente,

On bookes and on lernynge he it spente,

And bisily gan for the soules preye...

Sownynge in moral vertu was his speche,

And gladly wolde he lerne and gladly teche.'

[But all that he might get from his friends, he spent on

ooks and on learning,

And dedicatedly prayed for their souls...

His speech was constant with moral virtue,

And gladly would he learn and gladly teach.]

While the Clerk had his faults, he was Aristotle's philosopher for good old Chaucer, and through him, he was able to share his own ambition for himself: to be a lifelong learner and educator. I think Chaucer encouraged all his readers to follow that path — to be a seeker and giver of wisdom and knowledge."

"An Irish Blessing:

May you always have walls for the wind,

A roof for the rain,

Tea beside the fire,

Laughter to cheer you,

Those you love near you,

And all your heart might desire."

"Vladimir Nabokov: 'Curiosity is insubordination in its purest form.'"

"Do good recklessly."

"Proverbs 3:5–6: Trust in the Lord with all your heart and lean not on your own understanding. In all your ways, acknowledge Him, and He shall direct your path."

"Verily, with hardship comes ease." - Surah 94:5

"It's not the action but the reaction."

"Be the leader you wish you had." - Simon Sinek

"Not everything that is faced can be changed, but nothing can be changed until it is faced." - James Baldwin

"When God shows you the way, He will not let you down. He has your life, purpose, and your plans mapped out."

PART IV

Twenty Life Lessons From Dr. Kenneth Shore

1. Don't wish, do.

2. Let go of what you can't change.

3. It's the small moments that make life special.

4. Tell important people in your life how much they mean to you.

5. It is okay to be angry. It is never ok to be cruel.

6. Floss.

7. Do what scares you.

8. Stretch (I've never quite learned to do this).

9. Never buy what you do not want because it is cheap.

10. Spend some time alone.

11. Being kind is more important than being right.

12. Learn about your family history.

13. Don't be a pushover.

14. Become financially literate.

15. Stop at lemonade stands.

16. Fix mistakes quickly.

17. Pursue achievable goals.

18. Money and class are two very different things.

19. Telling someone he's wrong never leads to anything good — even if he is wrong.

20. Learn how to be handy.